In the shadows of the Himalayas - Legends from Vedic texts

Granthin Pubs

DEDICATED TO THOUSANDS OF YEARS OF

INDIAN TRADITION AND STORY TELLING

Shiva

Shiva stands out as the ultimate cool dude of the divine realm. A god with a blue throat because he once chugged a deadly poison to save the world. Shiva prefers meditating on chilly and tall mountaintops (maybe he's not a fan of beach holidays), and has a fashion sense that's, well, out of this world! He rocks a crescent moon in his hair like it's the latest trend and wears a snake around his neck as if it's the coolest scarf ever made. And let's not forget his ride, Nandi the bull. It's like his eco-friendly version of a supercar!

He's also known as the Lord of the Dance. His dance, named Tandava is actually super important—it keeps the universe in balance! Imagine if every time you did your happy dance, you were keeping the world in a good working state.

An important festival dedicated to Shiva is Maha Shivaratri. People stay up all night, sing songs, and tell stories to show their devotion for Shiva. While he is rarely angry, when made angry, he can open a third eye that can shoot fire to destroy evil. Best not disturb his calmness. Shiva teaches us some cool lessons: Be bold, be unique, and sometimes, just sitting back and finding your peace is the most powerful thing you can do.

Nandi

Meet **Nandi**, the divine bovine, Shiva's number one vahaan (ride) and the most blinged-out bull ever. With a coat that gleams like he's fresh off a carwash every day and a gaze so kind he could make onions cry tears of joy.

One day, Nandi had an epic idea. He was going to snag the prettiest flower in the entire forest, something so stunning it'll make Shiva's two eyes (not the third one) pop open in amazement. Nandi went on a floral treasure hunt, high-hoofing every critter he met. He saw flowers of all sorts - marigolds with more sass than a reality TV star, lotuses cooler than a cucumber at a spa, and sunflowers that could double as selfie sticks. But Nandi, our bovine botanist, believed he can do better.

Just as the sun was setting, Nandi stumbled upon a clearing where the air was practically glittering. And there it was, the floral equivalent of a unicorn, a bloom so dazzling it's like a disco ball in petal form. Nandi, picked the flower and took it back to Mount Kailash. Upon arrival, Nandi presented the petal extravaganza to Shiva. Shiva loved it and the flower got the VIP treatment in the celestial gardens, standing as an eternal reminder of Nandi's big discovery.

Parvati

Parvati, Shiva's companion, is like the forest's favorite teacher, loved by every leaf and critter. When she rocked up, the birds turned their tweets up to a concert level, and even the shyest critters would pop out for a quick "hello." But one bright and shiny  morning, something was not right. The forest was as quiet as a library on a Friday night. Parvati, curious and concerned, wandered deeper into the woods and found a scene straight out of a plant horror movie: trees with brown, sad leaves, and flowers drooping like they'd just watched a sad movie.

Parvati sat down right in the middle of this botanical boo-hoo fest and started to meditate. She wasn't just thinking happy thoughts; she was pushing out mega love vibes, calling on Earth's magic touch to perk things up. As she got her meditate on, a glow wrapped around her like a cozy blanket, and then, it started to rain. But this was no ordinary rain. It was like a magic potion shower, making everything it touched burst back into happy green life.

The forest folks, from the ants to the zebras, couldn't believe their eyes. Their home went from "blah" to "ta-da!" just like that, thanks to Parvati's green thumb and giant heart. And from that day on, the story of Parvati's super-powered love for the forest buzzed around like the bees, inspiring everyone to treat nature like their best buddy and help anyone in need, leaf, or petal.

Brahma

Brahma is known as the creator and the "singularity" from which the universe is born. When you have 4 heads, you tend to become creative. It's like he sat down with a giant box of LEGO bricks and thought, "Hmm, what should I make today?" Instead of building a spaceship or a castle, he decided to create the whole world! It's like he was the ultimate artist, painting with the stars and sculpting with the clouds. And the best part? He didn't even need to look up a tutorial on YouTube!

But here's a funny thing: even though Brahma created so many cool things, he sometimes forgot what he made! Imagine making a whole planet and then being like, "Oops, did I put too many mountains over there?" With four heads, you'd think he'd remember everything, but hey, everyone forgets where they put their keys sometimes, right? Brahma is not just about creating things and then stepping back. He also helps maintain the balance in the universe, and his work reminds everyone about the cycle of life, that everything has a beginning and an end, and then new beginning again, just like the seasons.

So, next time you're building something out of LEGO or drawing a picture, just think of Brahma. Who knows? Maybe you're a creator in the making, too. Just remember if you ever feel like you're forgetting something, you're in good company. with the four-headed creator of the universe!

Saraswati

Saraswati, the wife of Brahma is the goddess of wisdom, knowledge, science, and music. Imagine having a teacher who could also be a rock star! Saraswati was known for her dazzling white attire, which she probably chose to stay cool under the celestial sun, and her trusty veena, a musical instrument.

One day, Saraswati decided to host a talent show for all the celestial beings. Everyone wanted to showcase their talents, hoping to impress her. Even the moon wanted to participate, rehearsing a "moonwalk" that was quite literally out of this world. The sun put on its best glow; the stars twinkled in anticipation, and the planets aligned for the best view. The talent show was a hit, with acts ranging from meteor showers to constellations forming shapes of animals. Every year a festival called Saraswati Puja is celebrated in India. Students and artists pay respect to her, hoping for wisdom, creativity, and success in their endeavors. It's a day when books, musical instruments, and tools are worshipped instead of being used, showing respect for the tools of learning and creativity.

Saraswati teaches us that knowledge and wisdom are very important in life. She encourages us to always be curious and learn new things. Just like a good friend, Saraswati is there to guide and support us on our journey of learning and discovery.

Vishnu

Vishnu is a super awesome and important god who can transform into all sorts of forms to do incredible stuff for people. Think of him like the ultimate superhero whose main gig is to keep the universe in tip-top shape. Imagine being in charge of the whole universe—that's a huge job but hey, someone's got to do it, and Vishnu is on it with flair! He's often spotted lounging on a giant snake named Shesha, who floats on the cosmic sea. Shesha has got loads of heads and is really comfy, kind of like a magical floating mattress.

The most exciting part about Vishnu is his avatars. An avatar is like a divine character he takes on to come to Earth and sort things out when they get a bit too messy. It's like Vishnu has a wardrobe of superhero costumes for every kind of cosmic crisis!

The ten avatarsof Vishnu are Matsya; Kurma; Varaha; Narasimha; Vamana; Parashurama; Rama; Krishna; Buddha; and Kalki. The tenth avatar, Kalki is yet to be arrive.

He is usually seen with Lakshmi, the goddess of wealth and fortune, and often rides on the back of Garuda, a mighty eagle-like bird. In essence, Vishnu embodies the principles of order, right action, and compassion. Through his stories and teachings, he offers guidance on how to live a balanced and righteous life.

Garuda

Garuda isn't your regular, garden-variety bird who might peck around for worms. Garuda is like the superhero of the bird world, with mighty wings that could span the clouds and a dazzling presence that made even the sun do a double-take.

Garuda has an extra special role as the pilot for Lord Vishnu. Whenever Vishnu needed to zip across the universe to stop some cosmic mischief, Garuda was his go-to ride.

Garuda loved to play pranks on other gods. Imagine him sneaking up behind them while they were busy taking their selfies and photobombing them with his enormous wingspan, shouting, "Cheep-cheep, gotcha!" Garuda also had a bit of a sweet beak. No birdseed or berries for this king of the skies. Garuda was all about the celestial ambrosia, a divine nectar that was supposed to be for the gods. But Garuda, with his cheeky charm, would often swoop in and take a sip when the gods weren't looking.

So, the next time you see a bird soaring in the sky, give a little wave, who knows, it might just be Garuda on a secret mission, ready to swoop down and share a giggle or two.

Lakshmi

Lakshmi is the goddess of wealth, fortune, and prosperity. Lakshmi had a magical touch. With a wave of her hand, she could fill empty pockets with shiny coins and turn barren fields into bountiful gardens. She liked to see people doing good deeds, being kind, and working hard before she'd sneak up behind them and, "Surprise!" fill their lives with abundance.

She carries a conch, a discus, a lotus, and a pot of gold. The conch was for making music. The discus was like a frisbee for those super intense divine picnics. The lotus was because, well, who doesn't love flowers? And the pot of gold—let's just say she was everyone's favorite guest at parties.

On Diwali, the festival of lights, everyone would clean their houses, wear their best clothes, and make delicious sweets, all to invite Lakshmi in. So, if you were missing a couple of sweets from your plate, you knew Lakshmi had been there, and good fortune was sure to follow. So, remember, if you want Lakshmi to pay you a visit, be kind, work hard, and maybe learn to make some delicious sweets. Who knows? You might just find an extra gold coin under your pillow.

Jyoti

Lakshmi's ride isn't your standard fare; nope, she's got **Jyoti**, an owl so blinged out with golden feathers she could double as a disco ball. With peepers sharper than a detective, she could spot a good deed in a haystack of  naughtiness. Together, they're like the dynamic duo of delight, zipping around sprinkling joy and cash like fairy godmothers with a banking license.

As Diwali rolled around, the time when every LED and diya gets its moment to shine, Jyoti flapped her wings and took to the skies. Her eagle eyes, or should we say, owl eyes, zoomed in on a village that looked like it had been left off the guest list for the light parade.

Jyoti hustled back to Lakshmi to share the news. Lakshmi smiled and followed Jyoti to the village. With a wave of her hand, she showered the village in a soft, golden glow. The wilted crops in the fields stood tall and lush, the empty market stalls filled with goods, and the villagers' simple homes sparkled with new life.

From that day on, the villagers prospered, never forgetting the lessons of kindness they had learned. Perched on her tree branch like a feathery judge on talent show night, Jyoti's eyes sparkled with the satisfaction of a job well done.

Trimurti

Brahma, Vishnu, and Shiva are known as the **Trimurti** (The Great Trinity), and each had a very special role in the universe.

Brahma is the Creator, with four faces looking in every direction. He carried a book, a water pot, a spoon, and a string of beads. With his boundless imagination, Brahma shaped the stars, planets, and all living creatures. He loved crafting beautiful worlds and filling them with colors and life.

Vishnu is the Preserver, with a calm and kind demeanor. He had four arms, holding a conch, a discus, a mace, and a lotus. Vishnu's job was to look after all of Brahma's creations, ensuring harmony and balance. Whenever the universe was in trouble, he would descend in avatars, to restore peace and order.

Shiva is the Transformer, often seen with a crescent moon on his head and the Ganges River flowing from his hair. Shiva's role is to bring change by ending what was old to make way for the new. He dances the dance of destruction to clear the way for Brahma to create again, completing the cycle of creation, preservation, and transformation.

This great trinity teaches us the beautiful balance of creation, preservation, and transformation that exists in the world.

Ganesha

Ganesha is a beloved deity, with an elephant head, big friendly ears, and an even bigger heart! He's super smart and loves to help people, especially when they're starting something new like the first day of school or a cool art project.

He's known as the "Obstacle Remover"—kind of like a superhero who clears the path so you can skate through without tripping! His favorite snack is something called modaks, which are yummy like cupcakes. Plus, he has the cutest little mouse for a buddy and even rides it like a scooter—how fun would it be to zoom to school on a mouse?

Every year, people throw a giant birthday party for Ganesha that goes on for ten whole days. It's filled with music, tasty treats, and people makecreative statues of Ganesha. At the end of the party, they float these statues in water to send Ganesha back to his mountain home. It's like saying, "See you next year!"

Oh, and did you know Ganesha is also a mega bookworm? He once wrote a huge epic called the Mahabharata, which is packed with all sorts of great stories. But here's the cool part: when his ink pen broke, Ganesha didn't just give up—he broke off one of his own tusks to keep writing! That's how dedicated he was. It shows us that to do awesome things, you need smarts, courage, and to keep going even when it gets tough.

Mooshak

Mooshak is Ganesha's friend and vahaan (ride). A mouse with a coat as soft as the clouds and eyes that sparkled like the stars. His tiny feet could scamper fast, and his whiskers twitched with excitement for every new adventure.

One sunny morning, Mooshak was awakened by the sweet smell of modaks, Ganesha's favorite treat. He stretched his little legs, twitched his pink nose, and scurried out of his cozy hole to find the source of the delicious aroma. A group of children where sitting near a tree, one of the children, a little girl named Aanya, seemed upset. Her kite had gotten stuck in the branch of the tallest mango tree, and no one could retrieve it.

Fighting the urge to chase the smell of Modaks, Mooshak, with his whiskers twitching, decided to help. With the agility only a mouse possesses, Mooshik climbed the mango tree, his tiny claws gripping the bark firmly. The children watched in awe as the little mouse made his way up, higher and higher, until he reached the branch where the kite was trapped. With a few clever nibbles and tugs, Mooshik freed the kite. As he reached the ground, the children cheered.

As the sun set, painting the sky in shades of orange and pink, Mooshak knew that it was not just his size that made him special, but his big heart and brave spirit. And with Lord Ganesha by his side, a modak in his mouth, he was ready for any adventure.

Riddhi and Siddhi

Ganesha wasn't as successful in finding a partner to marry and he became the ultimate wedding crasher. Imagine, just as the divine wedding rituals are about to be exchanged, in struts Ganesha, tossing obstacles like confetti. The other gods, tired of rescheduling their divine nuptials, were in quite the bind. They decided to approach Brahma.

Brahma, the cosmic problem solver, had a great idea and thought, "Why not turn the teacher into the student?" So, he sent over his daughters, Riddhi (Ms. Fortune) and Siddhi (Ms Enlightenment), to learn under Ganesha, with a secret mission to keep his mischief in check. Picture them, the ultimate wing-women, perched by Ganesha's side, not just as symbols of wealth and wisdom but as covert agents.

Whenever word of a divine wedding wafted through the air, Riddhi and Siddhi would spring into action, distracting Ganesha with the cosmic equivalent of "Look, a mongoose!" Thus, the divine weddings could proceed without any issues.

But, Ganesha soon caught on to their tricks. But in a divine twist, Brahma, with a twinkle in his eye, suggested, "Why not marry the mischief away?" And so, Ganesha tied the knot with Riddhi and Siddhi, turning from the ultimate party crasher to a doting husband.

Rama

Rama stands out as a hero with a heart of gold and a sense of duty that's as unwavering as his trusty bow. He is known as "Maryada Purushottam". "Maryada" translates to honour and righteousness, and "Purushottam" translates to "the supreme man". Rama lived in the kingdom of Ayodhya, and, was known for his bravery, kindness, and his Maryada.

Rama's sense of duty took him on a grand adventure, famously known as the quest to rescue his beloved wife, Sita, from the clutches of the ten-headed demon king, Ravana. Along the way, Rama made some friends, including a devoted monkey warrior named Hanuman. One of the most important festivals associated with Rama is Diwali, also known as the Festival of Lights. It marks the day when Rama returned to Ayodhya after 14 years of exile and his victory over Ravana. People celebrate this day by lighting lamps, which symbolize the victory of good over evil and the light within us.

Rama is a symbol of virtue and righteousness. His life stories teach us about duty, honor, bravery, and the importance of staying true to one's values. He is a hero not just because of his strength in battle, but more so because of his kind heart, his respect for all living beings, and his unwavering commitment to doing what is right.

Sita

Sita is the all-star kid, born from the earth and raised by King Janaka. She was so nice that even the roses stopped to smell her! King Janaka threw a massive competition where the main event is trying to string a bow so big it probably had its own post code. Picture all these princes and muscle-bound warriors queueing up, puffing out their chests, only to find out they couldn't even budge this mega bow.

Enter Rama, this prince with the heart of a lion and the gentleness of a kitten. He catches a glimpse of Sita and thinks, "Wow, she is cool" So, he steps up, and guess what? He strings the bow like it's a shoelace, winning the challenge and making Sita go, "He's the one!"

But then, Ravana, the demon king thought he could crash this love story by kidnapping Sita and whisking her away to his lair. But Sita keeps her cool, betting on the good guys to win. Rama, with the help of Hanuman, and a band of fearless warriors. launched a mission that was so epic, it's been talked about ever since.

Hanuman

Hanuman is Rama's biggest fan and a super-strong half-human half-monkey, known for his big heart, even bigger muscles, and a tail that could do more tricks than a circus monkey on a sugar rush! Hanuman is the son of the wind god, Vayu, and Rama's number one helper, especially when it came to defeating the bad guys.

One day, when Rama's brother, Lakshmana, was hurt in a battle, Hanuman had to find a healing herb from a mountain far, far away. But when he got there, he couldn't remember which herb was the right one! So, what did he do? He didn't just pick one; he picked up the whole mountain and brought it back! Talk about taking "shopping" to a whole new level! His tail was like the coolest gadget ever. He could use it to leap over oceans, fight bad guys, or even as a cozy blanket on a chilly night.

So, boys and girls, next time you're out on an adventure, just remember be brave, be strong. And who knows? With a little bit of Hanuman's spirit in you, you might just be able to leap over your own oceans.

Krishna

Krishna, an avatar of Vishnu was known for daring deeds and playful pranks that made him the darling of Vrindavan, where he grew up. A young Krishna, with twinkling eyes would sneak into the village pantry to steal butter. But this wasn't just any butter; it was the creamiest, most delicious butter in all the and, carefully guarded by the village ladies. Yet, somehow, Krishna and his friends managed to outwit them, leaving behind the empty pots.

Krishna's flute was another source of his playful magic. He could make anyone dance to his tune, literally. Animals, peacocks, and even the river would sway to his melodious call. When Kaliya a monstrous serpent poisoned the river, making it dangerous for the villagers, Krishna decided it was time for some intervention. But instead of a fierce battle, He danced on Kaliya with such grace and rhythm that the serpent got dizzy trying to keep up. In the end, Kaliya said sorry, and Krishna, forgave him, turning the fearsome showdown into a lesson on forgiveness.

So, the next time you hear a flute playing or see a peacock dance, think of Krishna and the playful spirit he embodies. Remember, a little bit of mischief, mixed with kindness and courage, can make life's journey a delightful adventure.

Radha

Radha and Krishna were the unbeatable duo of Vrindavan, kind of like the peanut butter and jelly of friendships. Their bond was super deep—deeper than any secret hideout and way more colorful than the biggest box of crayons.

Together, they were the life of the forest party. They'd spend hours dancing, and singing tunes that could make any "no dancing" sign want to boogie. When Krishna played his flute, it wasn't just music; it was like a magic spell that made Radha dance so beautifully, her anklets tinkled like little bells talking to each other. Their happiness was so catchy that even the birds would stick around to chirp along, and the trees couldn't help but sway like they were doing the wave. Every creature in the forest, from the tiny bugs to the big old bears, would sneak in to watch these two besties spreading joy like confetti.

And as stories go, Radha and Krishna's epic friendship turned into a legendary tale, passed down from one generation to the next, reminding everyone that true friendship and love are the most magical things you can share.

Durga

Durga is the powerful superhero of goddesses, with many arms! Well, each arm held a special weapon, from magical swords that could slice through darkness to shields so strong, they could bounce off any boo-boo. Durga rides a fierce tiger, which is way cooler than any bike you've ever seen. Together, they were the unbeatable team of bravery and roar-some strength!

One day, a troublesome demon named Mahishasura started causing a ruckus. He was part buffalo but a huge troublemaker, and he thought he was unbeatable. Durga, with her tiger, her weapons, and her dazzling smile, decided it was time to teach Mahishasura a lesson in manners. The battle was like the most epic dodgeball game ever. Mahishasura would throw a curveball of trouble, and Durga would dodge, weave, and strike back with her lightning-fast moves. Durga fought Mahishasura in a fierce battle that lasted nine days and nights, and on the tenth day, she defeated him. This victory is celebrated every year as the festival of Dussehra, which is a very happy and colorful time in India, filled with dancing, and delicious food.

Durga is like a superhero who shows us how to be brave, kind, and to always stand up for what's right. She teaches us that if we're brave and mean well, we can jump over any hurdle—kind of like playing a super fun game of leapfrog!

Kali

Kali is known for her fearsome appearance and a unique look that turned heads wherever she went. With her tongue sticking out, she wasn't afraid to make funny faces, especially when she wanted to lighten the mood or scare away any negativity.

Once a demon named Raktabīja was being naughty. He loved making copies of himself every time a drop of his blood touched the ground. Kali arrived, dressed in a wild outfit of animal skins and sporting a necklace made entirely of skulls. With her tongue sticking out, she was ready for action. Every time Raktabīja's blood tried to drop to the ground and make more trouble-making clones, she zapped through the air like a superhero and caught each drop on her tongue. "No more duplicates for you!" she seemed to say with each catch. Thanks to her quick moves, Raktabīja couldn't make any more copies of himself. And that's how the day was saved from the multiplying demon! It just goes to show, sometimes you need a bit of wackiness to solve a big problem!

Kurma

The story of Vishnu avatar **Kurma** is one of a remarkable turtle that turned the world upside down – quite literally!

The gods and demons were facing a huge problem. They were churning the ocean to make the nectar of immortality. They were using the mountain Mandara as the churning rod and the great serpent Vasuki as the rope. However, as soon as they started churning, the mountain began to sink into the ocean because it was so heavy. Enter Kurma, the superhero turtle, with a shell stronger than the toughest rock and a can-do attitude. He swam to the bottom of the ocean, lifted the huge mountain on his back, providing a stable foundation for the churning. And so, the ocean was churned, and the nectar of immortality was secured, all thanks to Kurma's strength and spirit.

So, the next time you see a turtle, remember the tale of Kurma, the mighty, and utterly indispensable hero of the churning ocean. It just goes to show, you don't have to be the fastest or the loudest to make a big splash – sometimes, all you need is a strong back and a good attitude!

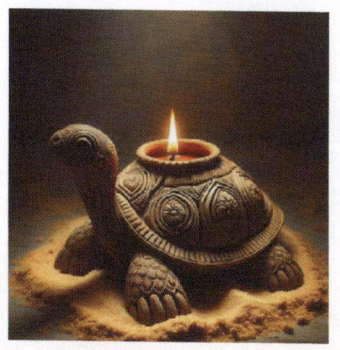

Indra

In the sparkling, cloud-kissed realm of the heavens, where gods and goddesses dine on ambrosia and swap stories of their divine deeds, there's one figure who often stands out for his thunderous presence. This is **Indra**, the king of the gods, a mighty figure known for wielding the Vajra, a thunderbolt as powerful as a cosmic electric shock, and riding on a magnificent white elephant named Airavata, who's so big, clouds are mistaken for his powder puffs!

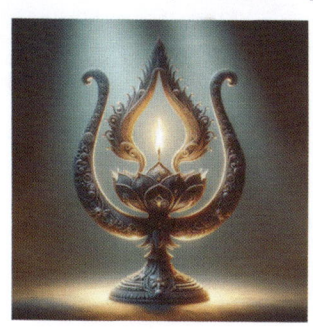

One evening, as Indra rode across the heavens, he noticed that a shadow had fallen across the land, a darkness that crept into the nooks and crannies of the world, stealing away the laughter of the rivers and the whispers of the winds. A great demon, Vritra, had cast a spell of darkness. Indra embarked on a journey into the heart of the darkness. The battle was fierce, a tumult of thunder and shadow, but Indra's light pierced the darkness, reaching the waters imprisoned by Vritra's spell. The land, once shrouded in silence, burst into a symphony of life, a testament to the victory of light over darkness.

Agni

Agni, the god of fire, really knows how to light up a room – quite literally! Agni with a flaming chariot is the divine equivalent of a cozy campfire, a warm hearth, and the master chef of the gods all rolled into one. Imagine having the power to roast a marshmallow to golden perfection just by looking at it. But it is not always simple, Agni, trying to help in the divine kitchen, accidentally turns up the heat a tad too high, and whoosh! The celestial cookies meant for an afternoon snack turn into little charcoal disks.

Agni is also known for his dazzling dance moves. The other gods have to remind him to keep the flames low, or they'll end up with singed eyebrows! "Keep it cool, Agni!" they'd laugh, as Agni tries to dial down his inner thermostat.

Through all his fiery adventures and warm-hearted jokes, Agni teaches us the importance of light in our lives – not just the kind that brightens our rooms, but the light of joy and laughter that warms our hearts. So, the next time you sit by a fire, watching the flames dance, think of Agni, the god who reminds us that a spark of humor can keep the fire of joy burning bright in our lives.

Vayu

In the world of legends, there's one character who's always in a whirl of his own – **Vayu**, the god of the wind. With a breezy personality and gusts of giggles, Vayu's tales are like a breath of fresh air, filled with fun and frolic. Vayu is the master of the skies, the commander of breezes, and the ultimate kite flyer! Imagine being able to control the wind – you'd never have a bad hair day, and you could send paper airplanes on epic journeys. That's Vayu for you, the celestial wind-whisperer, always ready with a puff to propel your hat into a merry chase.

Vayu is also known for his playful spirit, especially when it comes to autumn leaves. He loves to gather them up into mini tornadoes, making them dance and swirl like a leafy ballet. Vayu plays the role as the divine messenger, carrying voices and whispers from one corner of the world to the other. Sometimes, Vayu might playfully twist your words into a gentle breeze, making them tickle the listener's ear, turning serious messages into giggling whispers.

So, the next time you feel a sudden gust of wind, think of Vayu, the god who shows us that life is a breeze if we just learn to dance. with the wind, and the occasional tornado with a smile.

Shani

Shani is a cool deity with a dark and mysterious vibe, who chills out on a crow and wields a scepter like it's a magic wand. He's like the principal of karma and justice, keeping an eye on everyone's thoughts, words, and actions. Shani's also got a fancy title, "Lord of Saturn," the plant. He even has the best day of the week named after him—Saturday!

Legend has it that when Shani first opened his eyes as a baby, the sun decided to play hide and seek and whoops, we had an eclipse! Talk about making an entrance.

While his brother Yama waits until the afterlife to sort out the karma, Shani's more of a "no time like the present" kind, handing out karma cookies (both the good and the not-so-good kind) in this life itself. It's all about keeping things fair and square in Shani's cosmic courtroom!

Yama

Yama is the god of the afterlife. As the keeper of the afterlife, Yama has a big book filled with notes, doodles, and even the occasional funny remark about the deeds of mortals. "Ate broccoli for the first time – brave soul," Yama might scribble, next to someone's name.

Yama loves riding his magnificient and majestic buffalo called "Fluffy". Yama organizes quirky events like "The Underworld's Got Talent," where spirits show off their skills, be it ghostly singing or spectral dancing. Yama, with his hearty laugh and encouraging applause, makes sure everyone feels like a star. And let's not forget about Yama's annual "Bring Your Mortal to Work Day." It's a chance for the living to see the afterlife isn't all doom and gloom. With Yama as the tour guide, cracking jokes and offering free rides on Fluffy, visitors leave with a new appreciation for the afterlife and a lot less fear.

Yama teaches us an important lesson: that balance is key, even in the afterlife. He shows us that a sense of humour can brighten the darkest places and that even in the most serious roles, there's room for a little fun and laughter.

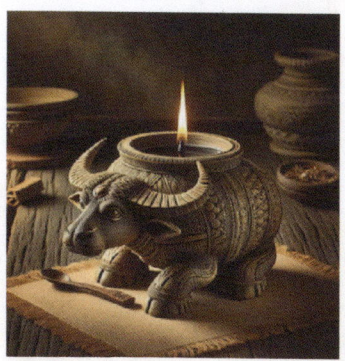

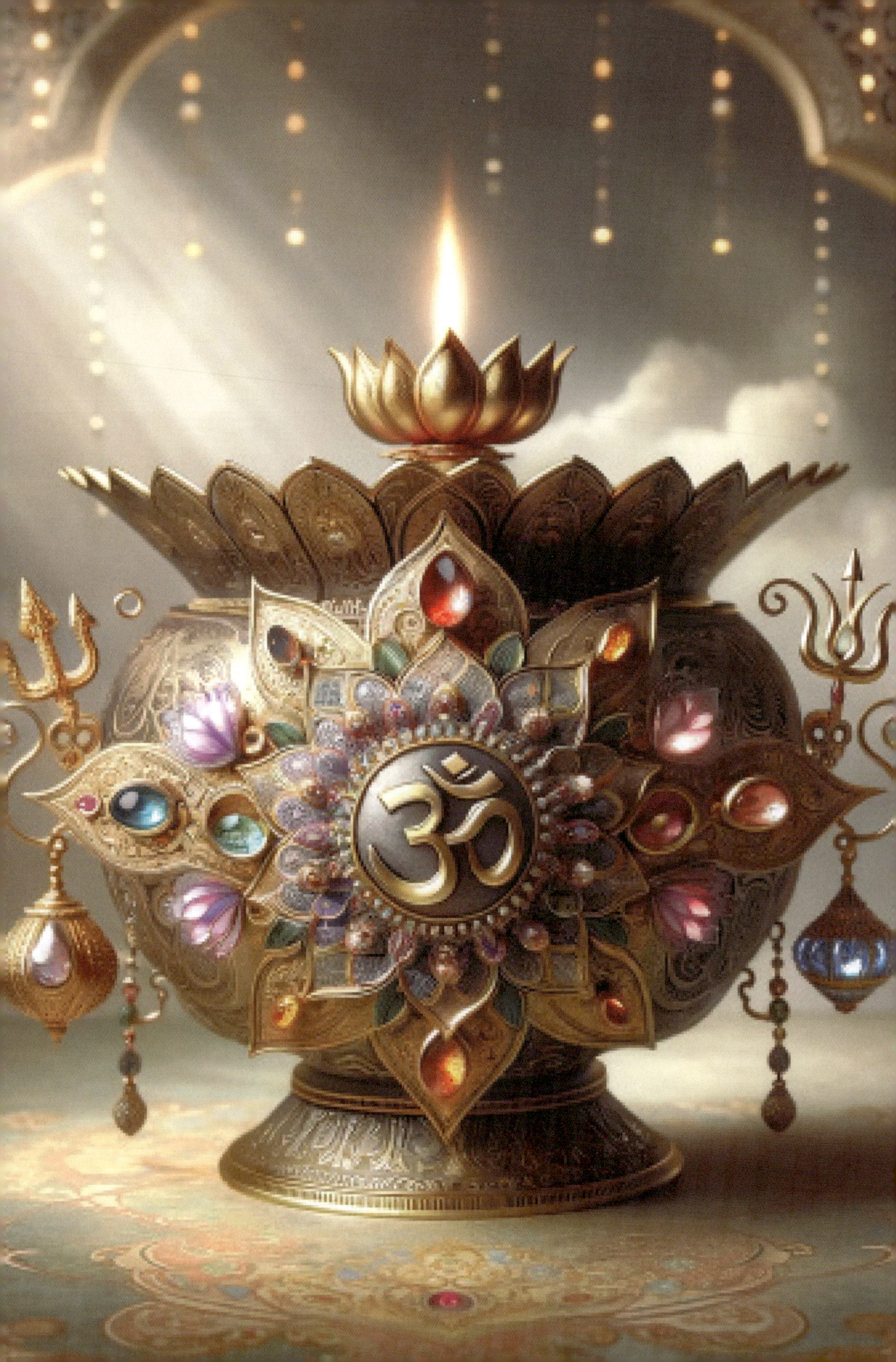

The gods and legends in this book are from Vedic texts and form a core part of Hinduism. Hinduism is a colorful religion filled with amazing stories and teachings that have been passed down for thousands of years.

Hinduism is also seen as a way of life that many people follow, especially in India. It's like a big adventure story with lots of amazing characters, just like in our favorite superheroes.

Overall these stories emphasize important values like honesty, kindness, compassion, and humility. They also teach us to treat others with love and respect, regardless of differences in background or beliefs.

Enjoy colouring these pages !

Enjoy colouring these pages !

Author : Granthin Pubs

Publisher : Granthin Pubs

Child Proofed by: Ved Iyer

Illustrator: AI (Dall-E)

SEND US FEEDBACK

We hope you liked our illustrations and narration of various legends from Vedic texts. To learn more about the publishers, the illustrator, their mission, other books and to send us feedback please visit

www.granthin.com

Books from Granthin:

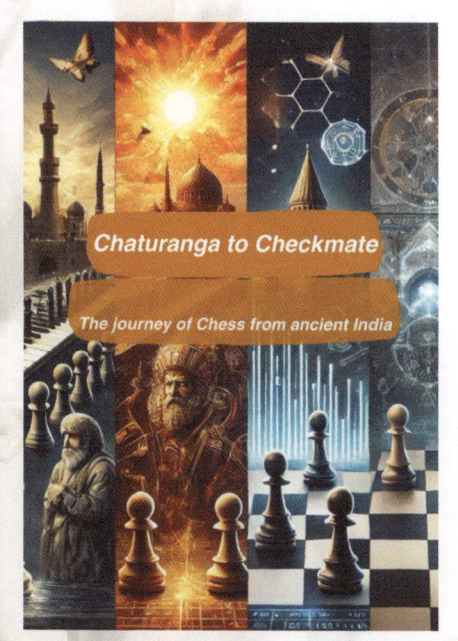

See www.granthin.com for links

Printed in Great Britain
by Amazon